1·2·3 Draw

Princesses

A step-by-step guide

by Freddie Levin

Peel Productions, Inc.
Vancouver, WA

Before you begin...

You will need:

- a pencil
- an eraser
- a pencil sharpener
- a ruler
- lots of paper (recycle and re-use)
- colored pencils for finished drawings
- a folder for saving your work
- a good light
- a comfortable place to draw

Now, let's begin!

Sparkle Alert!

When you see this symbol, you might like to add some sparkle to your drawing with a few drops of glitter glue or a shiny pen.

Library of Congress Cataloging-in-Publication Data

Levin, Freddie.
  1-2-3 draw princesses : a step-by-step guide / by Freddie Levin.
    p. cm.
  Includes bibliographical references and index.
    ISBN 978-0-939217-65-6
  1. Princesses in art--Juvenile literature. 2. Drawing--Technique--Juvenile literature. I. Title. II. Title: One-two-three draw princesses.
    NC825.P75L48 2010
    743.4'4--dc22
                            2009020975

Distributed to the trade and art markets in North America by

NORTH LIGHT BOOKS,

an imprint of F&W Publications, Inc.

4700 East Galbraith Road

Cincinnati, OH 45236

(800) 289-0963

Contents

REMEMBER:

1 Draw lightly at first (SKETCH!), so you can erase extra liines later.

2 The first few shapes are important. Notice the placement, sizes, and positions of the first shapes.

3 Practice, practice, practice!

4 Have fun drawing princesses!

Basic Shapes and Color Blending

Practice drawing these basic shapes:

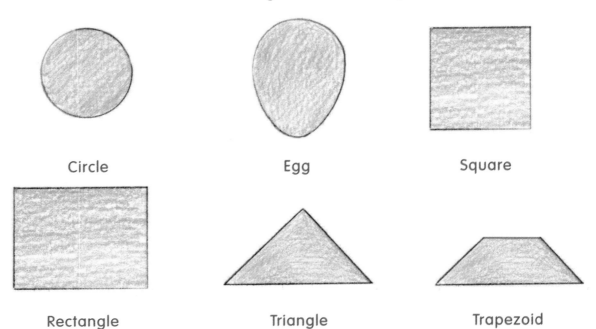

Circle   Egg   Square

Rectangle   Triangle   Trapezoid

Color and Color Blending

When putting the final shading and coloring on your drawing, start lightly. Add color slowly. Next to each example of a finished drawing, you will find small circles that show the colors used.

Try blending a little blue into the green and a little orange into the yellow. EXPERIMENT!

These are just suggestions. Please feel free to use any colors you wish. Princesses, like other people, come in every color, shape, and size.

Princesses - It's not just about the tiara.

These days the word 'princess' can have a very negative meaning. The image of a princess is often that of a spoiled, pampered girl who gets everything she wants or a pretty, passive young woman who is badly in need of rescuing.

However, the dictionary definition of a princess is just 'a daughter of a king or queen'. Many positive qualities can be found in the stories of princesses, both historic and fictional. Princesses can be kind, grateful, courageous, smart, curious, and even imperfect. They can be great warriors like Nzinga (page 45) or scholars like Eleanor of Aquitane (page 34). They can have hopes and dreams for themselves and their people. They can make a difference in their world. See page 63 for a reading list of stories that present princesses in a most positive way.

Note to parents and teachers:

Just like swimming, riding a bike, or playing the piano, drawing gets better and better with practice. Encourage children to practice drawing the basic shapes.

For very young children, or for children with poor motor control, cut the shapes out of tag board and let them trace around them. The size, shape, and position of the first few shapes are important. Once the beginning shapes and their positions on the page are established, the rest of the drawing can be built around it.

Basic Princess - Front View

A Princess is the daughter of a King and Queen.

1 Start with an egg and a trapezoid.

2 Draw eyes, a nose, a mouth, and eyebrows. Add two curving lines for the neck.

3 Draw two lines to begin the Princess's hair. Draw two long sleeves. Notice how they get wider at the bottom.

Are you remembering to DRAW LIGHTLY?

4 Add a tiara and the rest of her long hair. Draw the beginnings of her hands at the end of the sleeves.

5 Draw jewels on her tiara and add long hair lines. Draw fingers on her hands.

6 Add a necklace. Draw a star wand in her hand. Draw a sparkle design on her sleeves. Add a bow at her waist.

7 Draw her big, full skirt. Erase extra lines.

8 Add streamers to the bow. Put a sparkle design in the center panel of the skirt.

Shade and color your Princess any color you want.

Pretty Princess!

Add some glitter to the sparkle design on her sleeves and skirt. Add a little glitter to her wand.

Basic Princess - Side View

1 Start with an egg and a trapezoid. Notice the angle of both shapes.

2 Add an ear. Draw a nose, an eye, an eyebrow, and a mouth. The side view of a face is called a PROFILE. Draw two neck lines and the upper part of her arm.

3 Draw wavy lines for the Princess's hair. Add the lower part of the long sleeve. Add a rectangular shape to form the waist of her dress.

4 Add a pointed cone-shaped hat called a HENNIN. Draw her hand. Add lines to her waist to create a flared shape called a PEPLUM.

5 Starting at the point of the hat, draw a long, flowing scarf Draw a second sleeve. The Princess is holding a frog. Draw two ovals and a circle to begin the frog.

6 Draw the scarf and hair lines. Draw a second hand. Add the frog's eye and mouth. Draw an oval for his back leg and a line to show where it bends.

7 Add a ribbon and a bow to the waist of the dress. Complete the frog by drawing a back flipper and two front legs.

8 Draw a long skirt. Make it wider and curved at the bottom.

Shade and color your Princess.

Do you know the story of the Frog Prince?

11

Queen

A Queen is the mother of a Princess. She can be a ruler and also the wife of the King.

1 Start with an egg and a trapezoid.

2 Draw two eyes, two eyebrows, a nose, and a mouth. Add two curving lines for the neck.

3 Draw curvy lines for the Queen's hair. Add a 'V' for the neckline of her dress. Draw lines to begin the upper arms.

Don't forget:
SKETCH LIGHTLY AT FIRST!

12

4 Add a crown. Draw the lower arms. Notice the difference in the positions of the two arms.

5 She is wearing earrings and a ribbon with a medal. Draw these.

13

6 Look closely at this drawing. Starting at the top, add the crown jewels and draw the medal. Draw long sleeves and fingers on her hands. Add a long skirt. Erase extra lines.

7 Add stripes to the ribbon. Look at the diamond and line pattern on her sleeves and the hem of her skirt. Add this. Let's draw the King next. Then we can shade and color them together.

King

A King is the father of the Princess and the husband of the Queen.

1 Start with an egg.

2 Draw a trapezoid under the egg.

3 Draw an ear. Draw two eyes and eyebrows. Add a nose and a mouth. Add two curving lines for the neck.

4 Draw lines for the king's hair. Draw lines to begin the arms.

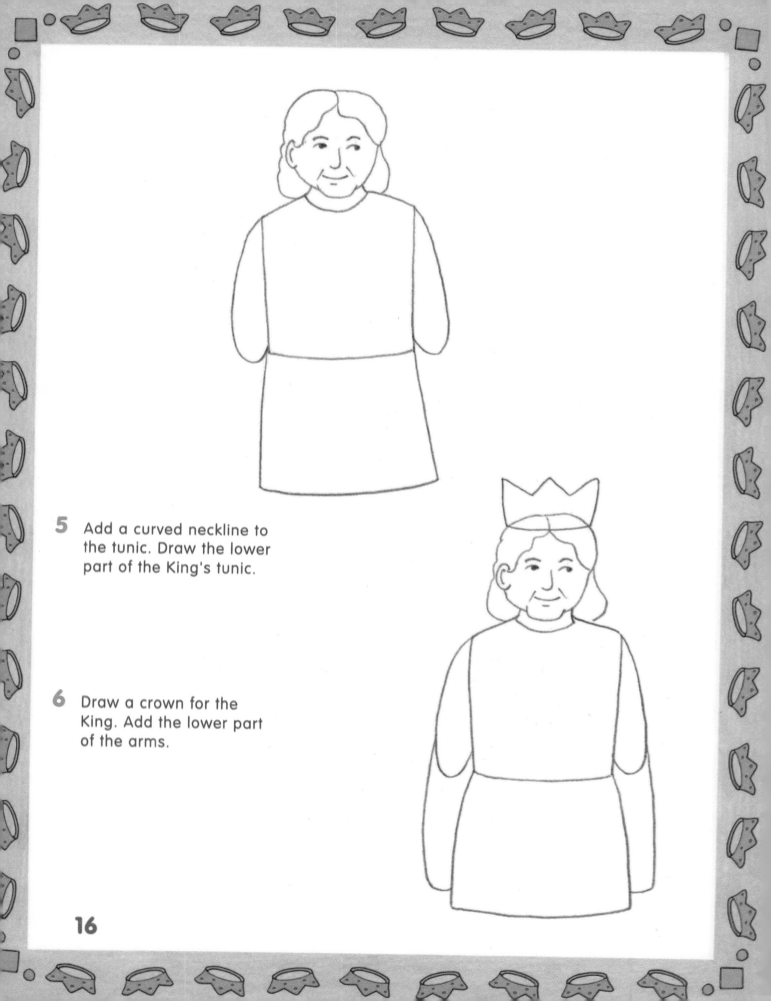

5 Add a curved neckline to the tunic. Draw the lower part of the King's tunic.

6 Draw a crown for the King. Add the lower part of the arms.

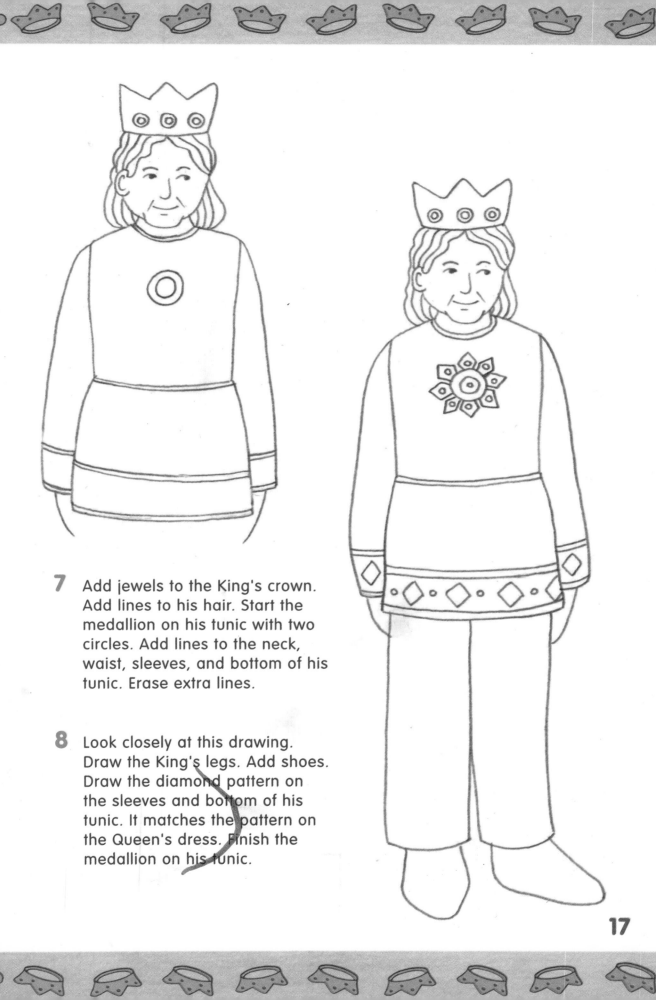

7 Add jewels to the King's crown. Add lines to his hair. Start the medallion on his tunic with two circles. Add lines to the neck, waist, sleeves, and bottom of his tunic. Erase extra lines.

8 Look closely at this drawing. Draw the King's legs. Add shoes. Draw the diamond pattern on the sleeves and bottom of his tunic. It matches the pattern on the Queen's dress. Finish the medallion on his tunic.

Shade and color the King and Queen.

Castle

The Castle is where the Royal Family lives.

1 Look closely at the beginning shapes. Draw a straight line on your page. Draw two rectangles. In between the rectangles, draw an arched doorway.

2 Add the tops of the TURRETS. A TURRET is a small tower. Draw two taller rectangles next to the first two TURRETS. Add four windows with rounded tops.

3 Add tops to the two taller TURRETS. Draw a taller rectangle in the middle above the doorway. Draw two more windows.

4 Draw three more towers in the back of the castle. Give each one a window.

5 Add tops to the three new TURRETS. Add flags flying on the tops of all the TURRETS. Draw the windowpanes in all the windows. Add a line to the middle of the door.

6 Look closely at this drawing. Add the details you see.

Shade and color your castle.

Cool Castle!

Tiaras

A tiara is a small crown for a Princess.

1 Start with an oval.

2 Draw a second line around the oval. Draw four triangles on the tiara.

3 Look at the butterfly and leaf shapes on the points of the Tiara. Draw these.

4 Add circles to the top of each butterfly shape and each leaf shape.

5 Shade and color your tiara.

SPARKLE ALERT!

Add some glitter glue jewels to your tiara.

6 Draw another tiara, Start with an oval. Add three teardrop shapes, with circles, on top. The center one is bigger than the side ones.

7 Draw two more teardrops next to the center teardrop.

8 Draw the last two teardrop shapes.

Shade and color your tiara.

Hat and Wand

Here is a pointy hat, called a HENNIN, and a star wand for your princess.

1 Start with a triangle. Notice the angle of the triangle.

2 Draw a curved line on the bottom of the triangle. This makes the triangle look like a cone shape.

3 Draw a long, flowing scarf on the hat. Add a rim to the bottom of the hat. Erase extra lines.

4 Shade and color your Princess hat.

5 Draw a star. Add a stick. Color your wand.

SPARKLE ALERT

Make your hat and wand shiny.

24

Prince

A Prince is the son of a King and Queen

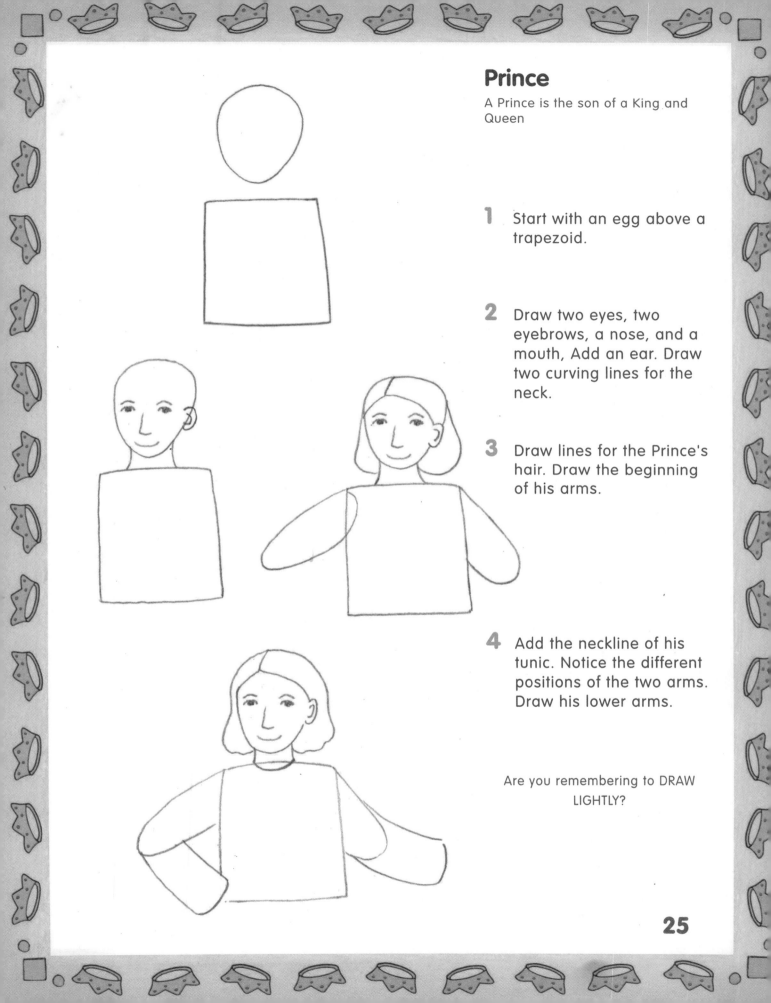

1 Start with an egg above a trapezoid.

2 Draw two eyes, two eyebrows, a nose, and a mouth, Add an ear. Draw two curving lines for the neck.

3 Draw lines for the Prince's hair. Draw the beginning of his arms.

4 Add the neckline of his tunic. Notice the different positions of the two arms. Draw his lower arms.

Are you remembering to DRAW LIGHTLY?

5 Draw a shield on the front of the Prince's tunic. Draw the beginning of two hands.

6 Draw the thumbs and fingers on each hand. Add the lower part of the Prince's tunic.

7 Draw the beginning of two legs. Erase extra lines.

8 Add hair lines. Draw the Prince's big boots.

Shade and color your Prince, and his shield.

The colors and symbols of family shields is the art of HERALDRY. The shield is called a COAT OF ARMS. Can you make a COAT of ARMS for your own family? You can learn more about HERALDRY at your school or public library.

Carriage

Your Princess can take a ride in her horse drawn carriage. First we will draw the carriage, then the horses. Then we will put both together.

1 Start with two circles connected by two curving lines.

2 Draw a smaller circle within the two circles to create a wheel. Add two little circles to make the center of the wheel. Draw two vertical lines in the middle of the carriage.

3 Draw a curved line, at the top of the carriage, and a straight line for the door and middle window. Look closely at the wheel spokes. Draw these. Add two curled lines above the wheels.

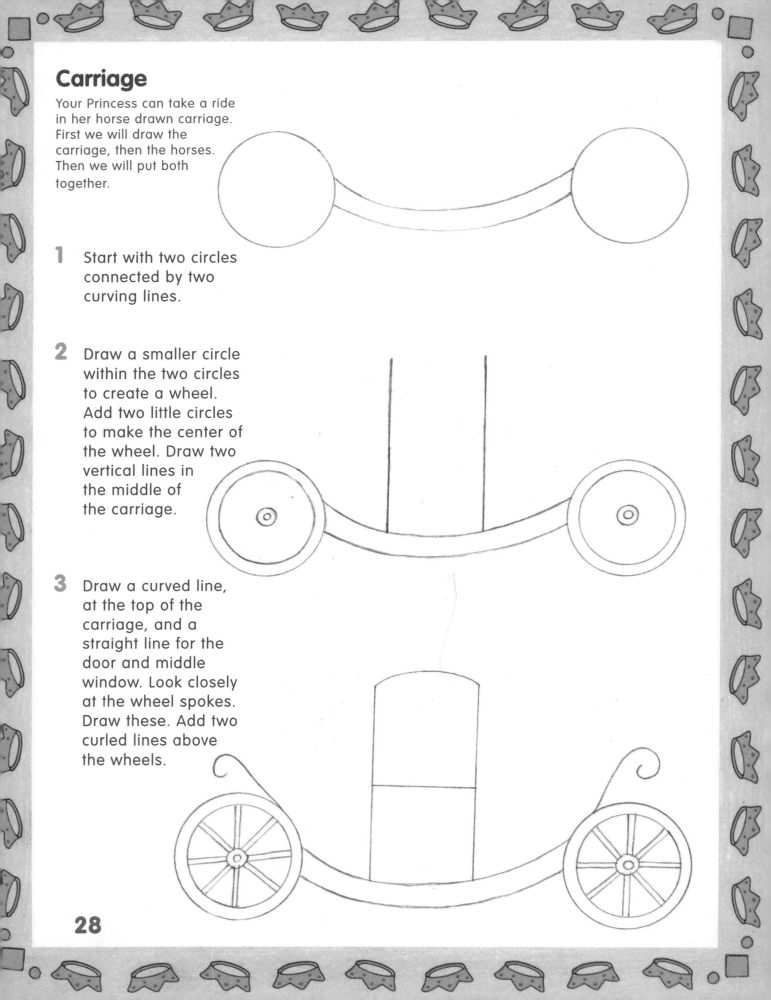

4 Draw the window in the center of the carriage. Complete the curly shapes at the front and back of the carriage. Add an oval on the door.

5 Look closely at this drawing. On top of the carriage, draw a straight line up and two curls on either side. Draw the two shapes on either side of the window. Draw the rest of the crown on the door.

6 Look at the curly lines on top of the carriage. Draw these. Add two windows on either side of the center window.

7 Finish the curls on top of the carriage. Draw two rectangles on either side of the windows.

8 Look at the final drawing. Add details you see. Finish the lamps. Add some lightly drawn lines in the windows to show reflections. The carriage is complete. Now let's draw the horses.

Horses

1 Start with three circles. Notice the positions of the circles.

2 Add two curving lines for the neck of the horse. Add a curving line for the back and one for the belly.

3 Draw two ears. Draw the muzzle. Draw lines to begin the four legs.

4 Add an eye and a nostril. Draw the second part of the legs. Add a tail.

31

5 Draw the horse's mane and tail. Draw the forelock on his forehead. Add a line across the muzzle. Draw the lower parts of all four legs.

6 Draw the rest of the horse's bridle. Draw the straps for the harness. Draw the hooves. Erase any extra lines.

7 Add lines to the mane, tail, and forelock. Add decorations to the harness.

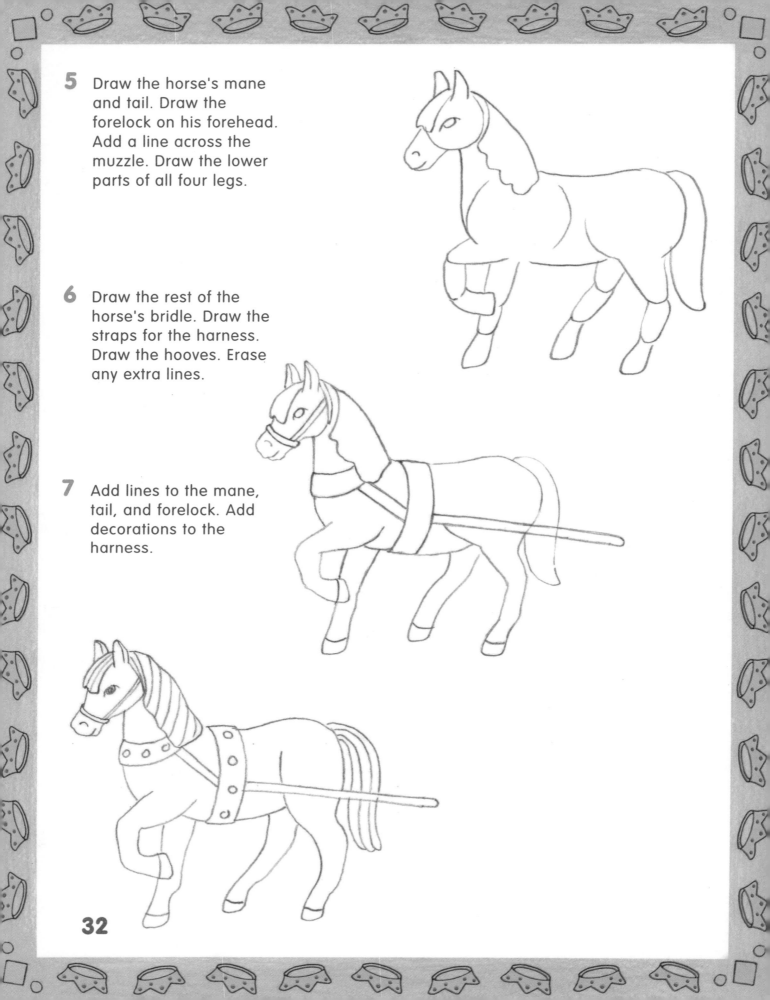

Shade and color your horses and carriage. Create a scene with a castle in the background.

33

Eleanor of Aquitane, Princess of France

Eleanor of Aquitane was born in 1122. She was the heir to one of the largest, richest provinces in France. Her father gave her the best possible education at a time when it was not fashionable to educate girls. Eleanor grew up reading and speaking Latin. She studied music and literature and was also excellent at riding, hunting, and hawking.

1 Start with an egg.

2 Add two eyes, two eyebrows, a nose, and a mouth. Notice the angle of the face. Draw two curving lines for the neck.

3 Draw a rectangle under the neck, to begin the body.

4 Draw Eleanor's hair lines and hat. Add lines to begin the arms.

5 Draw the curved neckline of her dress. Draw the lower half of Eleanor's right arm. Draw a curved 'V' shape to begin the book she is holding.

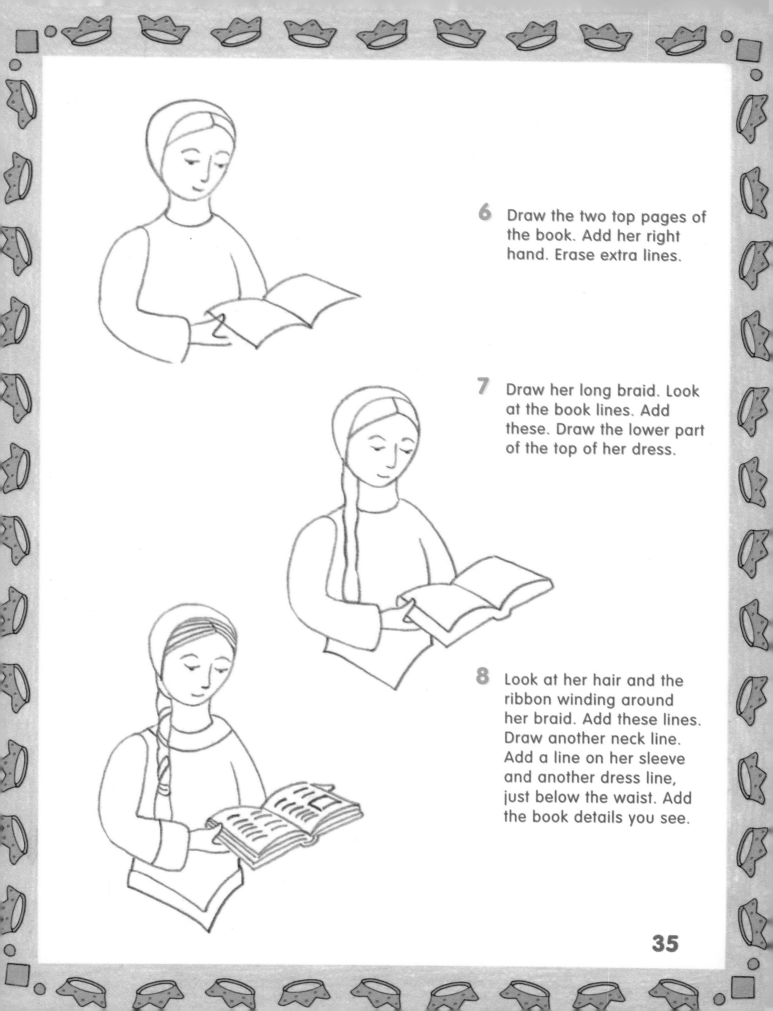

6 Draw the two top pages of the book. Add her right hand. Erase extra lines.

7 Draw her long braid. Look at the book lines. Add these. Draw the lower part of the top of her dress.

8 Look at her hair and the ribbon winding around her braid. Add these lines. Draw another neck line. Add a line on her sleeve and another dress line, just below the waist. Add the book details you see.

9 Look at her long skirt and ribbon. Draw these lines. Add additional lines to her braid. Draw extra lines to the neckline of her dress and around the edge of her sleeve.

Shade and color your portrait of Eleanor of Aquitane.

Elegant!

Nes Amun, Princess of Ancient Egypt

Nes Amun was the daughter of Ramses II, Pharaoh of Ancient Egypt, (1137 BC). Daughters of the Pharaoh often had their own palaces and great wealth. Nes Amun was educated and had religious duties as well. In this drawing, she is making a ceremonial offering with a golden cup on the banks of the river Nile.

1 Start with an egg and a trapezoid. Notice the angle of the egg.

2 Draw two curving lines for the neck. Add the upper arms.

3 Draw an eye, an eyebrow, a nose, and a mouth. Her face is in PROFILE.

4 Begin Nes Amun's golden necklace with three curved lines. Draw the second part of her arms. Notice the angle of her left arm. Erase extra lines.

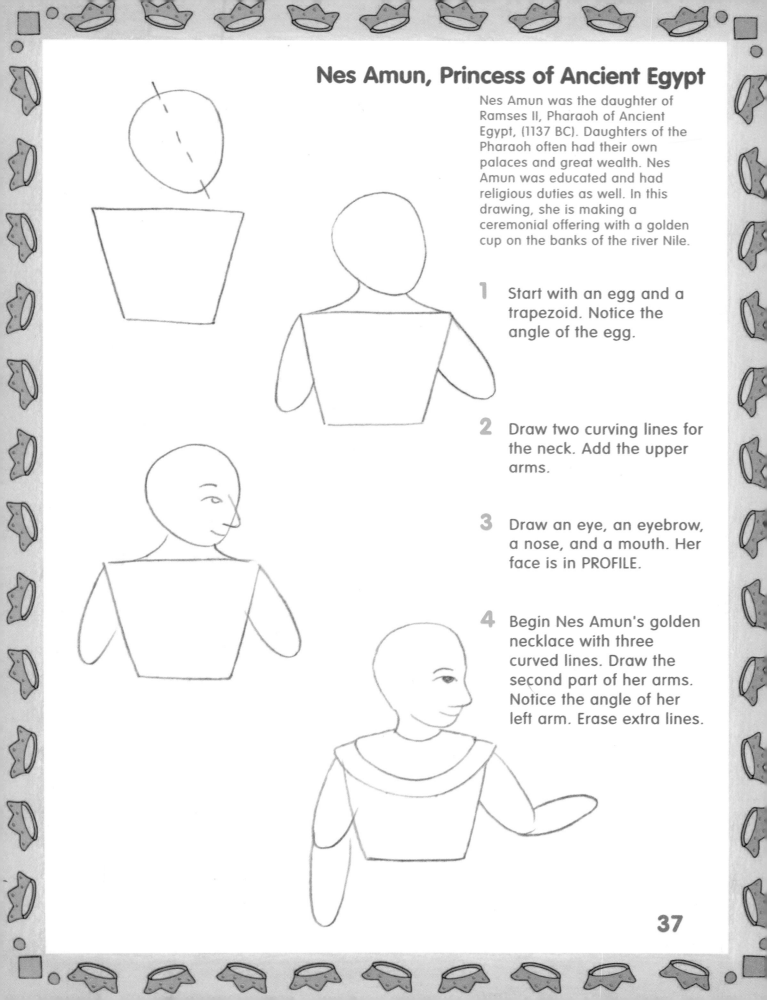

5 Look at the shape of Nes Amun's hair. It is actually an elaborately braided wig. Draw the outline of the wig. Add two hands.

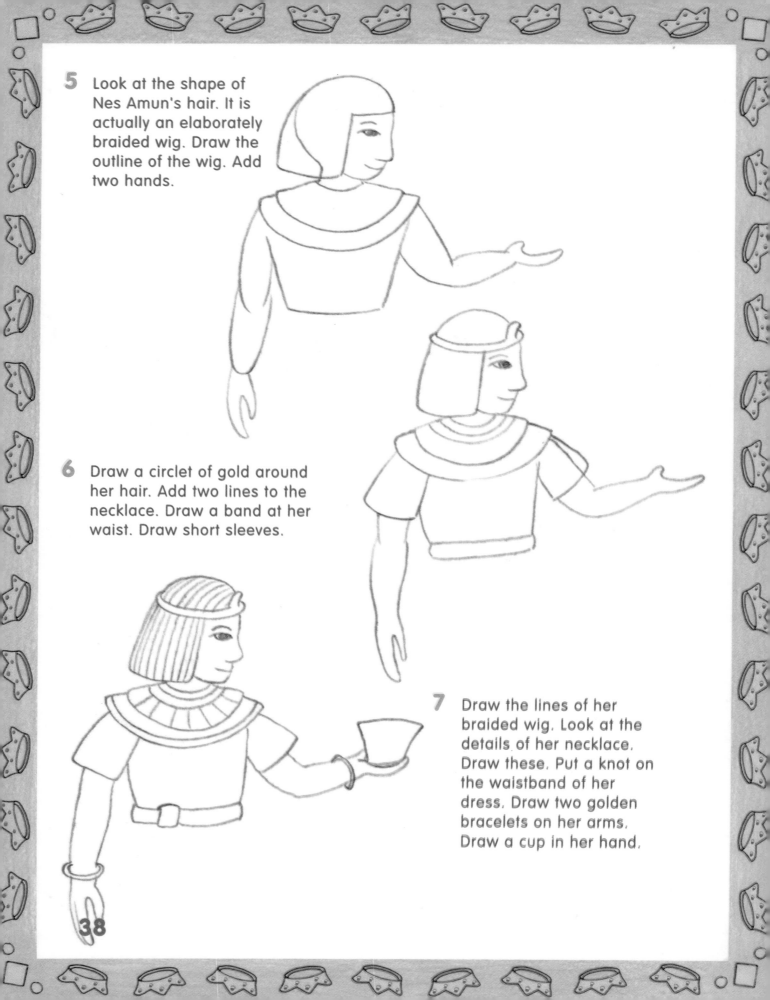

6 Draw a circlet of gold around her hair. Add two lines to the necklace. Draw a band at her waist. Draw short sleeves.

7 Draw the lines of her braided wig. Look at the details of her necklace. Draw these. Put a knot on the waistband of her dress. Draw two golden bracelets on her arms. Draw a cup in her hand.

8 Look closely at this drawing. Draw details on her necklace. Add her long skirt, legs, and feet.

9 Add more lines to the braids of her wig. Add lines in her skirt. Draw sandals on her feet. Add decorations to the cup. Add a pattern to the lower border of her skirt. Erase extra lines.

39

Draw Nes Amun on the
banks of the Nile River.

40

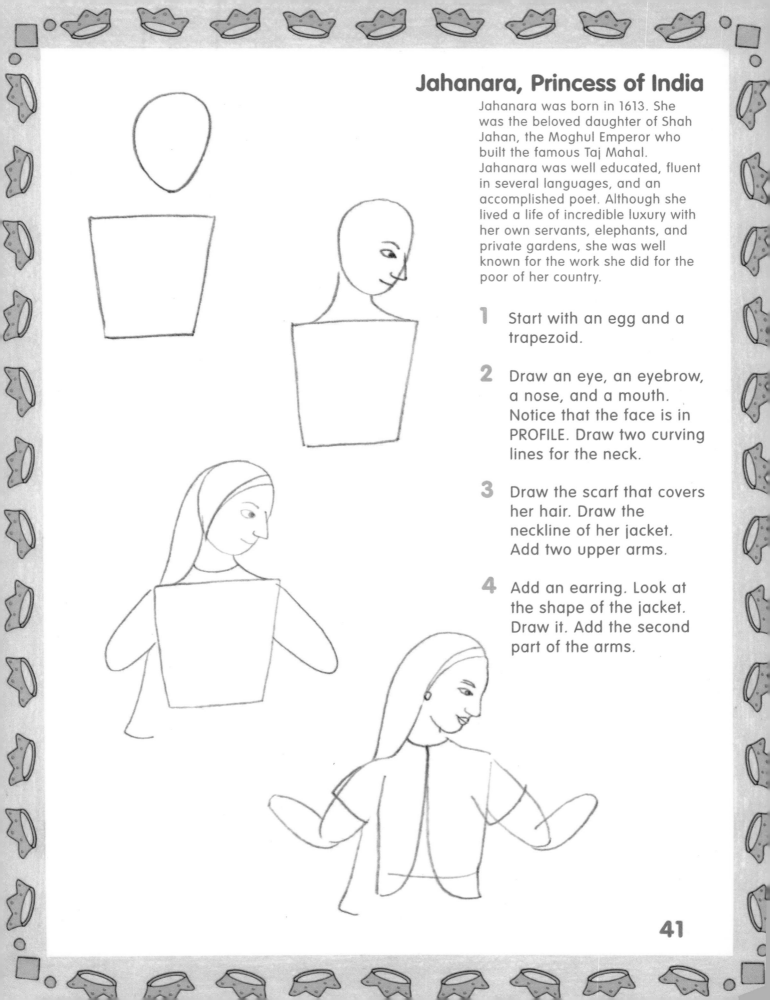

Jahanara, Princess of India

Jahanara was born in 1613. She was the beloved daughter of Shah Jahan, the Moghul Emperor who built the famous Taj Mahal. Jahanara was well educated, fluent in several languages, and an accomplished poet. Although she lived a life of incredible luxury with her own servants, elephants, and private gardens, she was well known for the work she did for the poor of her country.

1 Start with an egg and a trapezoid.

2 Draw an eye, an eyebrow, a nose, and a mouth. Notice that the face is in PROFILE. Draw two curving lines for the neck.

3 Draw the scarf that covers her hair. Draw the neckline of her jacket. Add two upper arms.

4 Add an earring. Look at the shape of the jacket. Draw it. Add the second part of the arms.

41

5 Draw the beginning of her two hands. Add the top of her skirt. Erase extra lines.

6 Look at her 'peacock' headdress. Draw it. Draw fingers. Draw the trim on the jacket. Add some bracelets.

7 Draw sparkles on the jacket. Add the trim to the upper skirt. Draw the rest of the skirt.

8 Draw her ankles and feet.

9 Look closely at the little bell details on her jacket and skirt. Add these. Add trim to the bottom of the skirt. Draw ankle bracelets and toes.

43

Jahanara lived in a beautiful palace filled with colorful mosaics. Shade and color Jahanara, and her palace.

SPARKLE ALERT
Add glitter to Jahanara's skirt and jacket.

44

Nzinga, Princess of Africa

Born in 1583, Nzinga was the daughter of the king of the Mbundu people of Southwestern Africa. Well educated by her father, she grew up to be a brilliant and courageous warrior who helped defend her people against Portuguese slave traders.

1 Start with an egg and a trapezoid.

2 Draw two eyebrows, two eyes, a nose, and a mouth. Add two curving lines for the neck. Draw the beginning of two arms.

3 Draw Nzinga's curly hair. Add the lower part of both arms.

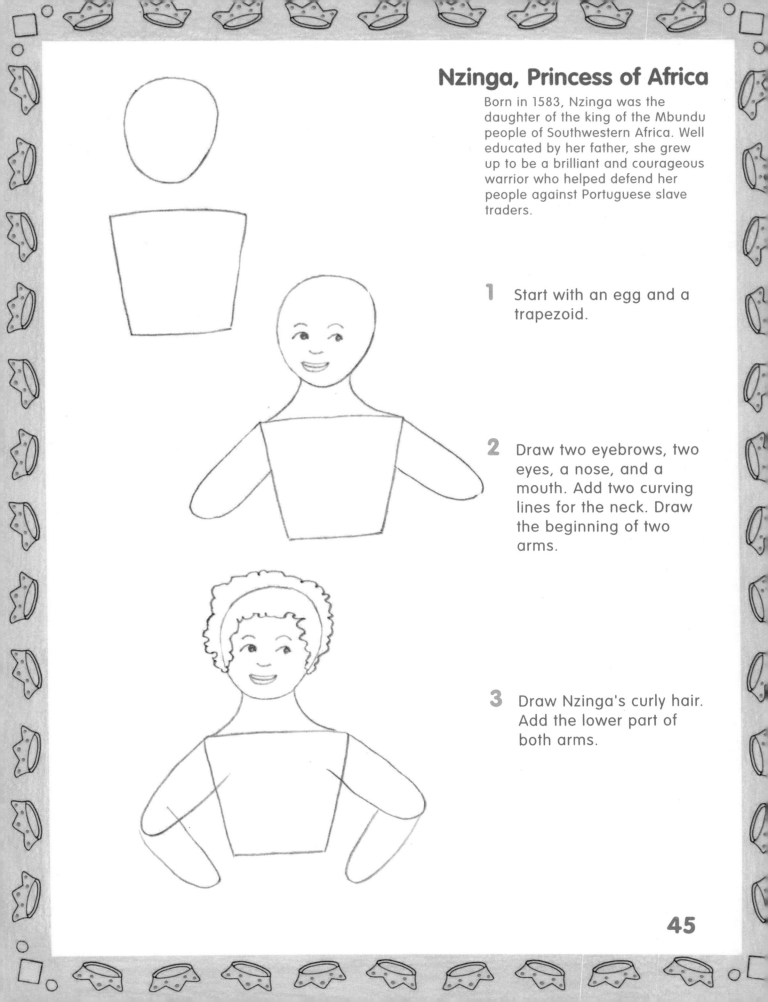

4 Look closely at Nzinga's posture. Draw her necklace. Draw a curved line for the top of her dress. Add the beginning of two hands. Draw her skirt. Notice that the bottom of the skirt is a wavy line.

5 Draw two bracelets around her upper arms. Draw her belt and the strap that holds her quiver of arrows. Add fingers to her hands.

6 Draw the top of the quiver that will hold her arrows. Draw her bow. Add the beginning of two legs. Erase extra lines.

7 Notice the strips wrapped around each end of the bow. Draw these. Draw Nzinga's feet.

47

8 Look closely at the additional details. Add these. Create a design for the top of Nzinga's dress.

Shade and color your picture of Nzinga.

48

The Sleeping Beauty, Ballet Princess

Aurora is the Princess in Tchaikovsky's classical ballet, The Sleeping Beauty, created in 1890. Dancers train for years to be able to perform this demanding role. This ballerina is dancing the Rose Adage, a solo in the first act.

1 Draw an egg and a trapezoid, to begin.

2 Draw two eyebrows, two eyes, a nose, and a mouth. Draw two upper arms. Notice the angle of the arms.

3 Draw the second part of both arms.

4 Look at her outstretched hands. Draw these. Add hair. Notice that her hair is pulled back in a bun.

5 Add fingers to the hands. Draw a tiara on her hair. Draw the top of her costume. Add the skirt to her costume. This kind of ballet skirt is called a TUTU.

6 Add lines to her TUTU. Draw the beginning of one leg.

7 Draw the lower part of the first leg. Draw her special shoe called a POINTE shoe. It's a specially made shoe that allows the dancer to stand on the tips of her toes. Draw the beginning of her other leg.

8 Draw the rest of her other leg. Add her shoes and the ribbons around her ankles.

Draw a ballet scene on stage.
Shade and color your creation.

Add glitter to her
costume and tiara

Turandot, Opera Princess

Turandot, an Italian opera written by Puccini in 1926, tells the story of a beautiful Chinese Princess with a heart of stone. Turandot demands that her suitors answer three riddles and if they fail - off with their heads! The ending is fairly happy (for an opera) and Turandot's heart is melted by love.

1 Start with an egg.

2 Draw two eyebrows, two eyes, a nose, and a mouth. Add two lines for a neck.

3 Draw a trapezoid. Add hair.

4 Look at her sleeves. Draw two sleeves.

5 Look at Turandot's headdress. Draw it. Draw both hands.

53

6 Add trim to the headdress. Draw a long skirt.

7 Add jewels to the headdress. Draw long lines to complete the front panels of Turandot's costume. Erase extra lines.

Draw an opera scene on stage. Shade and color your scene.

55

Fairy Princess

This Fairy Princess looks tiny because she is next to a big flower. Making an object in a drawing larger or smaller than usual is called changing its SCALE.

1 Start with an egg and a circle.

2 Add two eyebrows, two eyes, a nose, and a mouth. Draw two curving lines for a neck.

3 Draw two upper arms. Notice the angle of the arms.

4 Draw the second part of the arms.

5 Add the Fairy Princess's tiara and hair. Draw hands. Add her flower petal skirt.

6 Draw the Fairy Princess's long hair. Add a second row of petals to her skirt. Draw lines for her neckline. Erase extra lines.

7 Draw two antennae on top of her head. Add her wings. Draw the stem of her wand in her hand. Draw the beginning of two legs.

8 Starting at the top, draw hair lines. Draw the beginning of the flower wand. Draw two feet.

9 Complete the flower wand. Draw shoes on her feet.

Shade and color your Fairy Princess. Draw a flower for her to stand on.

Alien Princess

This Princess is from another world. Can you make up a name for her and her planet.

1 Start with an egg and a trapezoid.

2 Add two eyebrows, two eyes, a nose, and a mouth. Draw two curving lines for the neck.

3 Draw two pointy ears. Draw two long sleeves. Notice the angle of the ends of the sleeves.

4 Draw a crown. Add long hair lines. Draw a 'V' for a neckline on her dress. Add a belt around her waist. Draw long, skinny fingers.

60

5 Draw her skirt. Look closely at the final details. Add these.

Shade and color your Alien Princess.

Awesome!

Reading Princess

The Reading Princess loves to read and her favorite books are about Princesses! Check out her reading list. These books can be found at your public or school library. You can start a reading list of your own and add all your favorites.

1   Start with an egg. Draw the two covers and the spine of the book. Notice the angle of the egg shape.

2   Draw two eyebrows, two eyes, a nose, and a mouth. Draw the neck and the right arm, bent at the elbow. Add pages to the book.

3   Draw her hair. Draw the top of her dress and add two straps. Draw two hands on either side of the book.

4   Draw a tiara on her head. Add more hair lines. Look at the shape of the chair and arm rest. Draw the back of the chair. Draw the arm rest underneath her elbow. Add more pages to the book.

5 Draw the Princess's skirt.
Add the rest of the chair.

Shade and color your
Reading Princess.

Book List (For Reading or Being Read To)

The Paper Bag Princess by Robert N. Munsch
The Paper Princess by Elisa Kleven
The Princess Bride by S. Morgenstern
A Little Princess by Frances Hodgson Burnett
The Light Princess by George MacDonald
The Princess and the Pea by Lauren Child
Princess Ben by Catherine Gilbert Murdock
Princess Smartypants by Babette Cole
The Twelve Dancing Princesses by Marianna Mayer
The Tin Princess by Philip Pullman
The Princess Knight by Cornelia Funke

And many, many more....

63

Index